My tribute to Anne Boleyn.

From a Depression and Asperger Syndrome survivor.

Tim Price

chipmunkapublishing
the mental health publisher

Published by
Chipmunkapublishing
United Kingdom

http://www.chipmunkapublishing.com

I

Also by Tim Price,

Mental Health:
How to Improve Mental Health
Improving Care in the Community
The Changing World of Mental Health
My View of Mental Health Services.

Sport:
Olympic Games - London 2012
Olympic Games - Rio 2016
World Cup 2018
My Memories of Manchester United.

Miscellaneous:
My Insight into the World of Computers
My Middlewich.

My tribute to Anne Boleyn.

Introduction

I have always been interested in Anne Boleyn. She was a victim, in my opinion, of a political conspiracy and a royal desire for a male heir.

This book will give the reader a broader insight into my view of the life of Anne Boleyn.

A lot of the opinions are my own and not necessarily meant to be historically accurate.

In my opinion, the things she was accused of were almost certainly not true.

Anne's life was all too short but she gave birth to Elizabeth 1st, who was one of England's longest serving monarchs.

My interest in Anne Boleyn has been of some help to me in my mental health issues and my Asperger's syndrome. It has been a lifelong interest, I can identify with her and her struggles.

Overview

Anne Boleyn was married to King Henry the 8th. She was his 2nd queen, number 2 of the 6 wives of King Henry the 8th. I am very happy to write a new book about the life of Anne Boleyn. She was aged 35 when she was beheaded, she died on the 19th of May 1536. The things she was accused of when she died were almost certainly not true and because of the still born male air to the throne died when it was born king henry the 8th decided to go ahead and order the murder of Anne Boleyn. she was a faithful queen to henry the 8th. She was born in 1501. Her friend betrayed her and she became one of England best Queens of England. She died in London, England on the 19th of May 1535.

Anne Boleyn had a secret lover called Henry Percy who was secretly engaged to Anne Boleyn in 1523 but he did not acknowledge the engagement he was the 5rh earl of Northumberland and the relationship was broken off. Because he refused the engagement to Anne Boleyn.

Henry and Anne was formally married on the 25th of January 1533 a big day in the life of Anne and Henry the 8th.

Henry the king of England had Anne investigated for treason which was high treason in April 1536. On the 4th of May 1536 she was arrested and was put in the Tower of London. She was put on trial and before a Jury to be tried and she was found guilty and she was beheaded on the 19th of May 1536. It is 484 years since she was executed and beheaded it will be 500 years since her death in 2036 on the 19th of May 1536 I

As her daughter Elizabeth   became queen of England in 1558. She was a good queen of England. And Anne became venerated as a martyr of the English Reformation.

My tribute to Anne Boleyn.

Henry and Anne

Henry was not faithful to the queen. He married Jane Seymour soon after Anne was executed.

Anne should not had died at all she should have had a longer life time in Tudor England. She did not deserve to die or even be executed because I don't think she was guilty at all. The king was playing about with other women he eventually married 6 wives. He wanted to be in charge of the Church of England because the Pope would not agree to the annulment of his marriage to Catherine of Aragon. The monasteries should be still be standing the monks should be in the monasteries they have a life of prayer, every day.

Anne Boleyn has a lot of history about her life as the things she did were trueful to the trail on the 15rh of May 1535. I think that Anne Boleyn had a lot of potential to achieve during her life as a Tudor queen.

The Tudors had different way of living in public and private in the 1500 hundreds the life of the Tudors and King Henry the 8th. Was very different and Anne Boleyn her life was very short and she was a very different kind of person or queen she achieved a lot of things I don't think she craved the crown.

I did not realise she was the 2ndnd cousin of Jane Seymour the third wife of King Henry the 8th. The future of queen Anne Boleyn was a much more loyal queen of England but the things she was accused of was not true and the words she said was I take my leave of this world as I dedicate . My life and all of you and I heartily desire you to pray for me O lord have mercy on me to god as I commend my soul.

The daughter of King Henry the 8th and Anne Boleyn was one of the most famous queens after the lives of King Henry the 8th and Ann Boleyn.

The early life of Ann Boleyn, Who was Anne Boleyn?
Early Life

Anne's education was limited to arithmetic, grammar, genealogy, history, reading, spelling and writing. As was normal she was taught skills in dancing, embroidery, good manners, music, needlework and singing. Games she played included cards, chess, and dice. She would partake in archery, falconry, riding and hunting.

She was a daughter of Sir Thomas Boleyn and Elizabeth Howard. She was born in 1501, although there is some doubt about the actual year of Anne's birth. She had a short life in Tudor England because she was executed in 1536, aged a mere 35 years old. She was not ready to become Queen of England. Her relationship was not good with the king of England.

Europe

She went to the Netherlands and France to be educated in her early life.

Anne's father continued his diplomatic career under King Henry the 8[th,] in Europe and around the world Thomas Boleyn's charm was dominating Europe for the king of England which gained lots of admirers around Europe. Including Margret of Austria who ruled the Netherlands when Boleyn was there. She offered his daughter Anne a place in her household, ordinarily a girl of twelve years old would not gain such a position but she made a good impression with her good manners and her studiousness.

In France Anne was a maid of honour to Queen Mary and then to her 15 year old Stepdaughter Queen Claude and she completed her studies around Europe and the world of French customs. She developed interests in art and fashion and illustrated manuscripts of literature music and poetry and also gained experience in the French court, religious philosophy she gained knowledge in French.

Back in England

Anne came back to England in 1522 to marry her cousin James Butler but this did not take place. Anne gained a place at the Royal Court and she was awarded the post of maid of honour to Catharine of Aragon, Henry's first Queen.

In 1526 Henry became infatuated by Anne and began to pursue her seriously. He wanted to sleep her but she would not let him. She wanted to be married and therefore Queen of England. But Henry was already married to Catherine.

Annulment

It is probable that King Henry had thought of the idea of Annulment and divorce earlier than this as he strongly desired a male heir to accept the Tudor claim to the crown.

He really wanted a son but he did not get one with Catherine of Aragon.

Henry thought that Anne would give him a son, he was wrong.

Henry was not very loyal to his 6 wives before Henry's father Henry the 7th ascended his throne England was based some say that on civil warfare. There were rival claims to the crown of England and the king wanted to avoid a similar uncertainty over his succession.

Henry and Catherine had no living sons

All Catherine's children died, except Mary.

Anne saw an opportunity in Henry's infatuation with her and the convenient moral quandary, she determined that she would yield to his embraces only as his acknowledged queen. She began to take her place at his side in policy and in State. But not yet in his bed.

The royal Court went to a conference in Calais to try to get French support for the Annulment.

After returning to Dover Henry and Anne married in a secret Ceremony On the 14th November 1532 she soon became pregnant and to legalise the first wedding, considered to be unlawful at the time,

There was a second wedding service.

Thomas Cranmer, the Boleyn family chaplain, was appointed Archbishop of Canterbury. He declared the marriage of Henry and Catherine null and void. Five days later he declared the marriage of Henty and Anne

to be good and valid.

Queen

She was a great queen of Tudor England, in my opinion.
Catharine was formally stripped of her title as Queen and Anne
was consequently crowned queen consort on the 1st of June 1533
in a magnificent ceremony at Westminster Abbey.

With a banquet afterwards she was the last queen consort of
England to be crowned separately from her husband unlike any
other consort Anne was crowned with St Edward crown which
had previously only been used to crown a king, not queen.

She went through London in a procession with a white cloth of
gold and other expensive trimmings. The public were not
impressed.

Pope Clement was unhappy with the end of the marriage of
Catherine and very unhappy about the marriage to Anne.

The king became head of the Church of England breaking away
from Rome.

It was the start of the break away from the Catholic Church as the
king was in control of the church this took a lot of time to process
this change.

The beginning of the Anne Boleyn saga and the ultimate betrayal
of Anne by of the king of England and the beginning of the
accusations about Anne Boleyn. In my opinion She did not do the
things she was accused of, it was made up so the King of England
gave the go ahead of the killing and murder of Anne Boleyn I
think that it is a shame that this happened.

After a coronation took place as Anne began a really quiet
beginning at the king's favourite residence called Greenwich
Palace as they prepared for the new born baby the child was born
earlier than expected.

On the 7th of September 1523 along the way to receive the good
news of the baby been born between the times of three and 4 o
clock in the afternoon.

A girl was born Henry wanted an heir to the throne as he longed
for a son but this did not happen the girl was christened
Elizabeth who would become queen one day and reign as queen
of England for a long time.

Henry had a mother called Elizabeth of York. The birth of a girl
was a heavy blow to the king of England as the future king of
England should be a boy. The future role of the king of England
became quite reliant on having a son which did not happen with
Anne Boleyn, the queen of England.

My tribute to Anne Boleyn.

Since they were expecting a boy to be born but this did not happen what a shame this did not happen. The king of Tudor England The celebrations for the heir were cancelled   but the idea carried on the infant princess was given a great christening and Anne decided that Elizabeth would become queen of England. Mary, Henry and Catherine's daughter had her title removed From her servants position Henry relaxed his wife fears as the future   looked brighter and the threat to the king separating Mary as the future of the king and Catherine before sending her to Harfield House.

With Princess Elizabeth, the daughter of Henry and Anne. Elizabeth became a great queen.

Queen Anne was given a much larger staff to look after her and her daughter.

The death of Catherine of Aragon took place on the 8th of January 1536. It was an event for Henry and Anne to celebrate

King's Change of Mind

The King and Anne, as queen, enjoyed a pleasant start to their marriage. Anne Boleyn was very clever and her great policies about the world and Tudor England and Tudor politics. She enjoyed a great life and spent thousands of pounds and most famously made the world a better place to improve the politics of Tudor England.

Her life was very exciting and enjoyable to exploit the politics of the day. She was not aware that Henty was going to try Anne Boleyn with the accused items of the downfall and execution in 1536. The future looked brighter for Anne and the summer was spent in her favourite residence of power.

She was in charge of a massive court she spent a lot of money about the world and in the royal court before her accusations that she did not do I think she is innocent of the charges, in my opinion.

The queen was expecting a baby, was prepared for the excitement and was aware of the pregnancy might go wrong. The king was injured by been knocked off his horse. He was down for 120 minutes. A great shame over the accident that Anne became ill after l losing the baby.

Anne took a long time to recover from losing the baby as the world of Tudor England. And in the way the memories of her expecting a new baby Anne saw Henry the 8th third wife, Jane Seymour resting on Henry's lap. Anne had a long time relaxing and overcoming the loss of the baby the king was in a fighting tournament the beginning of the end of the marriage as a royal the marriage took a long time to overcome the marriage as Henry still wanted a son but this did not happen with Anne Boleyn.

The main blame was put on Thomas Cromwell after talking about how to try to convict Anne Boleyn to the accusations she did not do in my opinion. There was a conspiracy against Anne Boleyn so there could be accusations that where put. Together and to try to prove her accusations Thomas Cromwell betrayed Anne Boleyn. As her evidence was dismissed and the conspiracy against Anne was nearly proven in the eyes of those judging her. Through writing Anne tried to argue her point of view but the accusations were great to bear the issues of the day. Anne was taken to the tower of London Thomas pressed the accusations of adultery he stole and he had a lot of money for himself. Thomas Cromwell filled in the letters for the king of England as the accusations before the execution on the 19th of May 1536. were not true. She

died an early death in Tudor England what a shame this happened
a long time ago.

The accusations were adultery incest and treason I don't think that
this happened it was such a shame she died early than expected.
This was a tragedy

Thomas Cromwell put the accusations together, what a traitor   he
tried to get a conviction and to put Anne Boleyn to death he
succeeded in this, and what a mistake.

He denied Anne Boleyn by lying to the king of England. Who was
Henry the 8th.

It was ironic that Cromwell was later to be beheaded himself.

Accusations

Thomas Cromwell put together a detailed accusation of Anne's
adultery naming four men, Weston, Brereton, Norris, Smeaton and
her brother, George (incest).

On the 2nd of May 1536 Anne was arrested and was put in the
Tower of London by going through the court gate of the tower of
London. The gate was large and this led to the decision not to use
the traitor's gate.

Anne was so upset at her situation that she collapsed when she got
to the tower

She wrote a last letter to Henry but he did not respond. Anne never
saw Henry again.

Her life was cut short by the execution and her life was very short
in Tudor England.

She wrote a letter about her father and the one to the King of
England The letter concerned very important issues to do with her
relationship with the king and her marriage, she signed it as a
faithful wife.

The 4 people were given a trial in Westminster on the 12th of May
1536. Their denial and they prepared their innocence of the crimes
and the tortured person denied any wrong doing.

Three days after George Boleyn was tried separately in the Tower
of London. Before a jury of 27 peers she was accused of adultery
incest and high treason.

She was accused of adultery with five men, including her brother,
George.

I don't believe this ever happened at all.

11

I blame Thomas Cromwell a massive mistake and he betrayed Anne Boleyn. He did what the king wanted.

On the 14th of May Cranmer said that the marriage to Henry for Anne was void and null.

The End

The evidence applied to the men was not very strong but they were found guilty, sentenced to death and executed on 17th May 1536. The identifying of the people who had made friends with Anne Boleyn as she tried to be alive to she wrote to the king to try to survive without been executed. What a shame this did not happen. The execution should have never happened at all.

The way Anne Boleyn enjoyed her life and her life was cut short she had a shorter life than expected.

Anne was a good Queen of England. She went around the royal court and she was educated in France and the Netherland's. As a young child.

She was condemned to death by a jury of judicial peers.

Her impending death   may have made her upset before she was executed. And the suffering of her impending death took a long time for others to overcome her execution. The man in charge of the Tower of London (Constable of the Tower), William Kingston obviously spent a good deal of time with Queen Anne when she was imprisoned.

The date of her execution on the 19th of May 1536.

After the dawn of the day came she talked to Kingston to hear prayer with Anne Boleyn at a particular time in his daily day to day work of the king of England which was Henry the 8th.

On the daily work of her soul to salvation upon the Holy Sacraments but according to historians along the road to salvation. She was never unfaithful to the king of England in Tudor England. She did her daily routine in the royal household. Every day. She took the oath both immediately before she received the sacrament of her holy prayers of the day.

On the morning of the date of the 19th of May Anne was killed and executed within the tower precincts and upon the site of the execution. What a shame this happened

Henry commuted Anne's sentence Anne was very happy indeed and was ready to do with her life. From burning to beheading and rather have a queen beheaded with the common axe.

He brought in an excellent swordsman from Saint- Omer in France to perform the execution. On the 19th of May Kingston wrote a letter.

She died too early in my opinion.

Death and Burial

The ermine mantel was renowned   in the memory of Anne Boleyn and her beheading should have not gone ahead in my opinion what a shame it did happen.

Her headdress was quite colourful which was quite useful in her memory of the queen of England. the death of Anne Boleyn was so important in Tudor England and as the king ordered the murder of the queen of England. She died too early in my opinion in a brief farewell as the, memories of the queen of England dominating the Royal court of England and in Tudor England. As the request of the king and the crying ladies of the land as she was executed by a one stroke motion. As it was witnessed by the public in Tudor England.

The French executioner was quite good as the trade of his chosen field of work, he was swift at his work as the king got what he wanted.

He got rid of Anne Boleyn and she was murdered the king did not want her anymore.

The future looked bright for the king of England as he married his third wife after Anne Boleyn was executed what a shame that this happened.

She was buried in an unmarked grave in the Chapel of St Peter ad Vinucela.

Her skeleton was identified during renovation of the chapel in 1876 in the reign of Queen Victoria and Anne' s grave is now identified on the marble floor of the chapel.

My tribute to Anne Boleyn.

Remembered

There were unpleasant rumours, possibly started by someone called Nicholas Sander, that Anne had six fingers on her right hand. King Henry would have never had married Anne if it was true. These rumours were never correct in my opinion.

When they dug her up in 1876 nothing was found wrong. During her exhumation nothing was wrong with her fingers, she had 8 fingers and 2 thumbs, just like everybody else.

Anne Boleyn was very intelligent, gifted in musical arts and social pursuits. She was very strong willed and proud and often argued with Henry. Her biographer, Eric has eventually become dedicated to the cause of Anne Boleyn in her own personal life style.

To be openly inconsistent very religious and joyful and exciting and enjoyable person and never angry or even aggressive. To the origins of the Boleyn family. Or even calculating yet becoming emotional and exciting to be with and very strong person to be a great queen of England and Tudor England.

With the light of the day to improve relations with the king of England and of Tudor England. In 1536.

Anne was obviously a young woman of intelligence, spirit and courage.

The Change in Peoples Opinion: When Elizabeth Became Queen.

Anne Boleyn became a martyr to improve Tudor England and the way her exposure to the reign of the king of England, King Henry the 8th. She was thought of as the heroine who prevented Roman Catholicism in England.

Her powerful origins of the process of depending the Tudors in Tudor England. She was good queen of England.

I don't think that the accusations where true at all. Anne's life was very short indeed. She had a shorter life than she thought she would have in Tudor England.

She was a good follower of God and her religious beliefs where true to the origins of her life in Tudor England.

She was a great queen of England.

Elizabeth made sure that Anne was respected.

Elizabeth

The daughter of the King and Anne was educated as a Protestant, by Protestant scholars and she was prepared to be queen of England as the future of her legacy of her destiny she had no doubts about her capability to be queen of England after Henry the 8th died. Her ability to be queen of England was greatly appreciated as her ability to be queen was achieved as she became a great queen of England.

She was a great queen of England as her future following her father and mother as king and queen of England.

The evidence of her mother Anne Boleyn's guilt was very sketchy. Her great legacy of been queen of England after her father Henry the 8th died. She became a great and dedicated queen of England. She was her mother's daughter in different ways as she was in the Protestant religion as she was a great queen to remember her mother Anne Boleyn as the faith of Tudor England.

As the memory of the England spirit was quite real and her religious beliefs as the Protestant religion was followed quite well indeed.

As a young child her memories of Anne Boleyn was quite difficult to follow as her memories of been queen of England as the future was real to be queen of England.

She was born to rule Tudor England.

Tudor times and Tudor England where part of her origins to rule Tudor England and become queen of England after her father and mother died Anne Boleyn and Henry the 8th the king of England at the time of taking the throne after his dad died, the King of England.

Tudor England was quite different from other times of the royal family and the Tudors and ruling England. Anne Boleyn was one of the, most famous queens in Tudor England , she reigned supreme as the queen of England.

Elizabeth prepared for the throne of England after her dad died and the king of England and the king at Tudor England Elizabeth knew her mum was innocent but the murder still took place.

Elizabeth made sure that the population knew Anne had been wronged.

Elizabeth was very fond of her mother Anne Boleyn and her; loved her mother. Very much indeed.

Elizabeth was a great queen after Henry the 8th died and her mother died in 1536.

Elizabeth was protected to be preserved as a great queen of Tudor England.

After her dad and mother died king henry the 8th and Anne Boleyn Anne Boleyn was a great family member like her father Thomas Boleyn who owned a lot of land.

Anne Boleyn defended the royal realm of the Tudor England as she was a great queen of Tudor England.

Anne Boleyn was one of the most dedicated queen of Tudor England. She became queen of England and Tudor England she, married king henry the 8th.

Elizabeth adopted her mother's badge and motto, semper eadem (always the same). She restored Anne's legal title of Queen and her own as heir. She vindicated her mother. She even had a ring made which had portraits of Anne and Elizabeth.

In parliament she was one of the best queen of Tudor England. She was one of the best defenders of the royal realm in Tudor England as queen of England and in Tudor England.

She only reigned for three years as queen of England and in Tudor England.

Elizabeth restored Anne's legal title of Queen and therefore her own as heir to the throne.

She also appointed, or promoted members of Anne's family and friends.

It is therefore very clear that Elizabeth was well aware that her mother was innocent of the charges against her. To use a modern term, Anne had "been framed"

It was her father, Henry, who had wanted Anne out of the way so that he could proceed with his next marriage to Jayne Seymour.

Thomas Cromwell

Cromwell held many positions for Henry:

Commissioner of the Subsidy.

Master of the king's Jewell House.

Clerk of the Hanaper

Chancellor of the Exchequer.

Recorder of Bristol.

Steward of Westminster Abbey.

Lordship of Edmonton and several other places.

Surveyor of the King's Woods.

Principal Secretary.

Master of the Rolls.

Constable, jointly with Richard Williams of Hertford Castle and Berkeley Castle.

Visitor General of the Monasteries.

Steward. Duchy of Lancaster, Essex, Hertfordshire and Middlesex.

Steward of Savoy Manor Way.

Chancellor, High Steward and Visitor, Cambridge University.

Commissioner for the Peace, Bristol, Kent, Middlesex, Surrey, Essex, Derbyshire and Westmorland

Prebendary of Salisbury.

Receiver of Petitions in the Lords.

Lord Privy Seal.

Dean of Wells.

Vicar General

Warden of and chief justice, north of the Trent.

Governor of Isle of Wight.

Great Chamberlain.

And many more.

In 1527 Henry wanted his marriage to Catherine of Aragon to end so that he could marry Anne Boleyn. Cromwell manipulated Parliament and arranged for Henry to become Head of the Church of England. Cranmer declared the marriage of Henry and Catherine to be null and void thus paving the way for Anne's marriage to Henry.

Thomas Cromwell undoubtedly played a central role in Anne's story.

Thomas Cromwell was the main person to blame for the death of Anne Boleyn he first made her queen then framed her to get her executed, what a shame this happened.

Thomas Cromwell did the Kings bidding, he became the person to authorise the killing of Anne Boleyn so that the king can carry on and marry his third wife, Jane Seymour,   of the 6 wives of Henry the 8th.

Henry continued to pursue what he wanted to do and Cromwell let Jane Seymour become his third wife. This should have not happened at all in my opinion. The murder of Anne Boelyn was against the royal charter and the reason why Anne Boleyn died was in vain as she was murdered so that he could marry Jane Seymour and become his third life as the story of the 6 wives of Henry the 8th.

Anne Boleyn was betrayed by Thomas Cromwell who was the king's chief Adviser.

He was one of the main reasons why the execution of Anne Boleyn which took place on the 19th of May 1536.

The nearest modern figure to Thomas Cromwell is Dominic Cummings, Boris Johnsons Chief adviser. Who was kept in his job by his employer who is Boris Johnson he was not sacked as I think he should have been because he did not follow lockdown rules properly. He would have fitted in nicely in Henry's court.

Anne had a lot of enemies in the royal court and she was very successful in defending herself.

Cromwell was one of the most successful as chief adviser to the king of England and in Tudor England.

Cromwell became the main reason why Anne Boleyn was executed and killed on the 19th of May 1536.

He plotted and succeeded in getting Anne downfall in Tudor England.

He eventually became one of the king's great chief adviser.

The future of Thomas Cromwell was going to plot the downfall of Anne Boleyn and the queen of England and the queen at Tudor times.

He was one of the king's great defenders of the royal realms of the land.

The future looked bleak in the queens own life as the downfall of Anne Boleyn was not properly processed and the issues of her execution should have never have happened at all. What a shame this occurred on this day of reckoning.

The way Anne became Queen of England in Tudor England was quite different from other kings and queen of England and around the 15th century during the reign of King Henry the 8th.

Thomas Cromwell was the main person who plotted the downfall of Anne Boleyn and he succeeded in doing this exercise and got the execution to go ahead.

I think that this should have nor happened in the first place.

The downfall of Anne Boleyn was so exceptional in my opinion the execution should have not have gone ahead.

The downfall of Anne Boleyn took a long time to deal with the way Anne Boleyn was executed

The king got impatient because Anne did not give him a son and he was attracted to Jane Seymour. The chief adviser did what the king wanted him to do.

Anne was accused of adultery with Frances Weston, William Brereton, Mark Smeaton, Henry Norris and her brother.

Thomas Cromwell engineered the execution of Anne Boleyn and he succeeded.

Cromwell's end

Thomas Cromwell arranged King Henry's marriage to Anne of Cleves. The King had been told that she was a great beauty but when he saw her face to face he was shocked that she was very plain.

There was also a lot of pressure from aristocratic enemies.

Cromwell was arrested on 10th June 1940.

Cromwell was condemned to Death and without trial and properly beheaded on Tower Hill. On the 28th of July 1540.

Anne

She was born in the year of 1501 (there is some dispute about the date) and was the daughter of Sir Thomas Boleyn. she died in 1536 she was charged by Thomas Cromwell . She was not guilty of the charges, in my opinion, she was a dedicated wife to the king of England.

She was faithful to the king. The king of England was not he was messing about with other women, including Jane Seymour, his eventual third wife. 3 other women who were married to Henry. He eventually married 6 wives and they were called the 6 wives of King Henry the 8th.

The life of Anne Boleyn was so controversial.

Henry was denied an Annulment from the Roman Church, he broke from the church to marry Anne. She gave birth to a daughter and because she did not give Henry a son.

Because he was stillborn. The baby would have been heir to the throne.

She lived in France when she was younger and she was part of the Boleyn family, she was she had a sister called Mary .Thomas Boleyn was one of the Kings loyal servants.

Anne's father Sir Thomas was very interested in politics and the King's greatness, protecting the king of England who was Henry the 8$^{th.}$ $^{The\ King}$ he decided to destroy the monasteries what a massive mistake in the life of Henry the 8th king of England and the Tudor king of England.

The king of England at the time of Anne Boleyn who became his wife his second wife of his great friendship with the 6 wives of henry the 8th. The king was disloyal to Anne Boleyn she had other women in his courtship of the way the king married 6 women who became his wives and the history books said that they were all married to the king of England in Tudor England.

The King of England married Anne because he wanted to marry her after divorcing his first wife Catharine of Aragon. he wanted to be segregated from the Church and the separate from the roman church the way she went along her life early on before she became queen of Tudor England. She had a different. Kind of life style and her family owned a lot of land. Thomas was interested in politics and Sir Thomas was very loyal to the king of England King Henry the 8th.

He was not very loyal to Anne Boleyn. He was interested in other women. Over the years. He was one of the most famous kings of

Tudor England and he had a different way of living in Tudor England and the way she became his wife and queen of England and she was accused of things she did not do I think she should have had a longer life if she did not die in 1536 in London, England. She is one of my favourite people and she had a different kind of history when she was younger she was living in France for a long time before becoming to England and court King Henry the 8th he was disloyal to Anne Boleyn he chased other women which he married another three women. Who would become his three other wives he had been married to 6 wives they were called the 6 wives of Henry the 8th.

The life and times of King Henry the 8th took a long time before 1536 when Anne Boleyn died on the 19th of May 1536 what a shame a very short life in Tudor England.

The way she lived her life in Tudor England was to try to improve King Henry the 8th life and she was a dedicated wife to Henry the 8th. And the land she owned from her father sir Thomas Boleyn for the title and to be called a nobleman in Tudor England.

She was very different kind of person who eventually to become queen of England and the way she went along with things ad her life was short lived as queen of England and henry the 8th second wife. And the history of the family and making the land more valuable belonging to her father Sir Thomas Boleyn and the world around the family of Tudor England.

The future role of Anne Boleyn and her legacy of the way she was in the favour of the king of England she dedicated life to the king of England Henry the 8th.

He was on horseback doing lots of jousting and hunting along the royal woods of Tudor England, Henry was knocked off his horse and was unconscious. He never really recovered from this very nasty accident. Henry eventually married 6 women who would become his wives and the history books would say about the 6 wives of Henry the 8th. They had very hard lives to follow in the king's favouritism and the way the clothes where of gold and silver henry preferred women over girls I think that his life should have been more faithful to Anne Boleyn a long time ago. She tried to get a male air to the throne but her daughter was eventually queen of England Elizabeth who would rule Tudor England for a long time, after Henry and Anne Boleyn death.

The life of Anne Boleyn
The life Anne Boleyn had before she married the king of England
was quite different from when she became queen of England the
times where different under Henry the 8th. He was changing the
women and he gets tired of being married to Anne Boleyn the
queen of Tudor England.

The times of Anne Boleyn
The times of Tudor England and how to be queen where quite
different from the times of the father of king Henry the 8th. And
the life of Anne Boleyn and her dedication to the king as the
accusations where not true at all, in my opinion.
The life and times of Sir Thomas Boleyn who had   owned a lot of
land as rewarded for the loyalty to the king of England. King
Henry the 8th. The land was fought over as the land was given as a
present from the king of England as the land was now part of the
Boleyn family ownership of the land they owned over the years.

The future role of the Boleyn Family.
Anne Boleyn had a lot of land given by her father sir Thomas
Boleyn.
The family owned a farm and their property and land was very big
as Thomas was very loyal to the King.
The land made them very rich/

The times of the Boleyn sisters in France and in Tudor England.
The time spent by Anne Boleyn in France been educated and
learning the language of France.
The sisters got on with each other over the years. They shared their
time in France and also access the channel in Tudor England.

The times of political life in Tudor England.
Sir Thomas was a political person defending the king of England
who was Henry the 8th. His loyalty to the king of England was
very special indeed. As the king gave him more power to defend
the king of England.

The times of the Boleyn family and dedicated to the royal realms of the king of England who is Henry the 8th.

The Boleyn family had a great history of been loyal to the king of England and Tudor England as they defended the royal realms of the land and the project to enjoy life and defend Britain and England and in Tudor times. Of been very loyal to the king of England. And getting more land to acquire about the history of the family called the Boleyns and defending the royal realms of the land of Tudor England. The land was good and was part of the Boleyn family legacy and the world of Tudor England and the realms of the land and the changing roles of Sir Thomas Boleyn.

The world of Anne Boleyn

She started courting the king of England and the way the royal realms of the royal family and the way Anne Boleyn accepted her courtship with the king of England and the way she enjoys been part of the court and committee and Anne was very young lady to court King Henry the 8th the way she enjoys going to Hampton Court.

Sir Thomas Boleyn was in charge of the royal Household and after becoming in charge of money to finance the king of England in Tudor England.

The changing role of the Boleyn family

Anne Boleyn was dedicated to the king of England

The Boleyn family owned a lot of land over the years and the time taken as the fortune was made by means of political strife and the years as the memories of her father Sir Thomas Boleyn dedicated to the king of England who was Henry the 8th.

Sir Thomas Boleyn was very loyal to the king of Tudor England. The king of England was not very loyal to Anne Boleyn and he was after other women in the future of the way Anne Boleyn was to be queen of England and around Tudor England.

Anne Boleyn dominated the royal court of the way Anne was dedicated to the king of England and to Henry the 8th.

The role of Anne Boleyn in the royal realms of the Hampton Court the royal palace of King Henry the 8th.

She was a different kind of person and different kind of queen to marry Henry the 8th. During the rising against the Roman Catholic Church.

The rising against the Roman Catholic church and very different from the times of Tudor England. And Tudor England as the king was different from his father before Henry became king of England and became Henry the 8th. The king reign was different from when his father was king.

The way Anne Boleyn went about her life led to her marrying Henry the 8th and the role of the royal realm.

Anne Boleyn – Rumour and Reputation

Thomas Boleyn, Anne's father, was a diplomat and a very rich man.

Anne Boleyn did not have 6 fingers on her hands, it was a Catholic propaganda. She was one of the most controversial women some people called a witch, bitch, temptress but she was a real woman to grace Tudor England. We don't know the truth of many rumours about her. But we do know there was her fate to grace the royal court in Tudor England.

There is not portrait of Anne as there is of Henry the 8th. But she is said to have been a beauty and when she arrived at the court she was 21 years old. Apparently wise and dedicated to the royal realms the land. Anne was attracted to henry who at the time was in his prime, 6 foot 3 inches tall broad, chested in his prime. He was a musician and well respected as a good jouster.

He wanted a son which was not possible with Kathryn who had many babies but only one, Mary, survived

Henry was apparently very promiscuous with many mistresses, including Mary Boleyn but he had to change when he met Anne. He fell for Anne Boleyn, sha was very friendly but but she would not go to bed with him. Anne was in charge at this point I the relationship.

She wanted to marry Henry but they could not get married because he was already married. So with the help of Cromwell he became the head of the Church of England.

His marriage to Catherine was annulled and eventually Henry and Anne where married.

The Roman Catholic Church were not happy, they could not understand how the King of England could marry the daughter of a diplomat instead of a princess, who was Spanish.

But Henry could do what he wanted because he was head of the Church of England.

Anne Boleyn miscarried a male foetus on the same day that Catharine died.

Henry thought that Anne would not be able to give him a son again. She would probably have more miscarriages.

Henry became attracted to Jane Seymour, one of Anne's ladies in waiting.

He wanted her as his next wife.

But he was already married to Anne.

He eventually got Thomas Cromwell to do his bidding.

By accusing five men to of having an affair with Anne.

So she was taken to the tower of London.

Where she was accused of Adultery, Treason, and incest.

And so Anne was beheaded by an excellent swordsman from France.

My tribute to Anne Boleyn.

But this was an act of Kindness by Henry because her death would have been very quick.

King Henry the 8th was not very loyal to Anne Boleyn he was after other women he married 3 more women who became his 6 wives. Her life was very short. She had a life that was destroyed by king henry the 8th and he murdered Anne Boleyn by ordering the beheading.

Anne Boleyn was very loyal to the king of England and did not deserve to die.

Anne Boleyn
Most important points

The way Anne Boleyn is inspiring the world. She is definitely the one, from the six wives, who is the most famous, for obvious reasons.

The way Anne Boleyn went about her business in Tudor England, becoming queen of England and marrying Henry the 8th.

She had a short life in Tudor England after she became queen.

Anne Boleyn inspired the protestant world in Tudor England

The way she went around the royal court of henry the 8th.

Anne was so dedicated to the king of England.

She dominated the royal court but Anne was very loyal to the king of England.

The world of Anne Boleyn was complicated.

Anne Boleyn became queen of England and improved the world.

The role of Anne Boleyn in England's history.

Her great domination of Tudor England and after becoming queen of England.

Anne Boleyn and her father Sir Thomas Boleyn were part of the royal household.

Anne Boleyn courted the king of England who was Henry the 8th.

She went to the royal court and proved her loyalty to the King.

She was one of the greatest queens.

She became queen of England in 1533 she was queen for three years and she was one of the most dedicated Queens England.

She became one of the greatest queens of England.

She married Henry the 8th after the divorce of his first wife Catharine of Aragon

Her reign was cut short by her execution on the 19th of May 1536 by the order of the king.

She dominated the Royal court.

She wrote a special prayer book before she was executed on the 19th of May 1536. This should have never had happened at all. In my opinion.

She was educated in France and the Netherlands when she was a young child. She spent some time abroad been educated during her early life.

She graced Tudor times.

She became one of the best queens of England.

Places associated with Anne Boleyn that I would like to visit
It would be really good to walk the places and see the things she did as I want to remember her as a good queen of Tudor England.

My tribute to Anne Boleyn.

I hope to visit these places one day.
And also to celebrate her life on this earth and as queen of England.

Blickling Hall, Norfolk

Anne was born in this hall. The original Boleyn family home.
It is unclear exactly when because of the lack of records.
She did not stay long but moved to Hever Castle which is in Kent.
Blickling is said to be haunted by a headless Anne and by her father Thomas.
The hall does not exist anymore but there is a replacement on the same site.

Hever Castle, Edenbridge, Kent.

She lived in this castle, the new family home.
She was born at the original hall, Blickling. She was born to be queen of England in Tudor times.
Anne grew up in Hever, it was her home when she was a little girl.
Today there are a lot of things associated with Anne and her family.
You can see the famous portraits of Anne Boleyn, King Henry the 8th, Catherine of Aragon, Catharine Howard, Jane Seymour, Anne of Cleves, Catherine Howard and Catherine Parr. You can even see Anne Boleyn's personal prayer book with the words "The time will come, I Anne Boleyn" but in French probably because that is where she was educated and spent a lot of time.
When Anne was murdered Henry stole the castle and gave in to Anne of Cleves.
The reign of king henry the 8th was not a great time during the Tudors he failed to have a son as and heir because he died still born. So he ended up not having an heir to the Tudor throne.
It is also possible to see examples of armour, instruments of torture and execution.
Visitors have the chance to see the gardens and the lake.

Hampton Court Palace

This magnificent palace by the Thames near London in Surrey was once the home of Cardinal Wolsey but Henry seized it and made Hampton court his home when Cardinal Wolsey   lost his job.

It is still there and it is possible to see lots of rooms that Henry and Anne would know. The great hall and the great kitchens can still be visited.

I have been to Hampton court palace (it is enormous) but it was when I was younger and I would like to go back one day.

The palace was taken over by Henry the 8th with his second wife Anne Boleyn.

The great hall was built by Henry the 8th.

Queen of England and the way she became queen took a while to marry Henry the 8th.

Anne Boleyn became the mistress of Hampton Court Palace.

The Tower of London

The Tower is also by the Thames in central London. I went there when I was younger and I remember the beefeaters and the ravens. I intend to go back one day.

We went to the tower of London as a family.

It was started after the Norman Conquest by William the Conqueror.

Anne stayed at the Tower before she was married. There was a lavish procession on the River Thames prior to the ceremony.

Anne was imprisoned in the tower of London   after her arrest and was the first English queen to be publicly executed.

Anne was tried and for treason, incest and adultery in the Lieutenants Lodgings of the tower of London. And her ghost is said to haunt the queen's house , which was not built until after her death.

 She was then executed on the 19th of May 1536. On Tower Green. She is buried in the Church of St Peter ad Vincula.

She should not have been executed or died early in my opinion because she was innocent of the charges, in my opinion.

She had an early death than expected she had a great life as queen of England an on the date of Anne Execution which was the 19th of May 1535 this is the man dominating the reign of King Henry the 8th.

Thomas Boleyn died in 1579 a long time after the execution of his daughter Anne Boleyn this should have never have happened.

Anne was tried for treason and the accusations where not true.

And her life was cut short as her reign as queen only lasted for about three years before she was executed on the 19tth of May 1536.

My tribute to Anne Boleyn.

She was killed by been executed on Tower Green on the 19th of May 1536.

She is buried within the tower walls at the church of St Peter ad Vincula.

She also had a lot of potential, as queen of Tudor England, to be there for years.

I intend to visit the Tower, see the rooms and walk in Anne's footsteps

She was one of the most famous queens of Tudor England and the reign of the king of England Henry the 8th.

She dominated the royal court and defended the royal realms of the land during Tudor England.

She was one of the greatest queens of England but her reign was very short as queen of Tudor England.

I have always been very interested in writing a new book about Anne Boleyn and to also to promote mental health as well

There needs to be a new book about the Queen and Anne Boleyn and how she became queen of England. This is the book.

I have written a new book because about I wanted to write something different instead of writing about mental health the queen and why I think she is innocent of all the charges in my opinion. And Anne Boleyn.

I also wanted to try to sell my books to different kinds of reader's not just about mental health and write a new history book.

Writing this new book about Anne Boleyn has helped me through Lockdown.

I have really enjoyed writing this new book about my opinions of Anne Boleyn and how she died on the 19th of May 1536.

The time will come Anne Boleyn.

These words are most famous words of Anne Boelyn she said them in her Prayer Book.

At Hever Castle you can see several portyrts of anne Boleyn and the king of England Henry the 9th.

They are most famous of the king of England and Hnery the 8th.

They are painted by some famous painters around the time of Anne and Henry the 8th.

The domating years of her short reign as queen of England only lasted three years as her life was very short because she was tried for treason and adultery as the queen of England in Tudor times and in tudor England.

She graced the world and she became queun of England in 1533 only to be killed and executed on the 19th of May 1536 she was found giuilty but I don't really beleave this happerned at all in my opinion.

I think anne Boelyn was killed two early as her ;life as queen was cut very short indeed as she should have reigned as queen of England for much longer than about three years. As queuen of England.

But this did not happen as her life was very short for some reason this is a shame this happerned in the first place.

The life and times of Anne Boleyn

The life and times where quite different from tduor England and in Tduor times as life time was very different forom other queens of England and tudor times where quite hard to follow during her short regin as the queen of England.

The times and life of Anne Boleyn where quite hard to follow as the way the queen of England and in Tduor times.

The reign of king henry the 8th was quite hard after becoming king after his father died henry the 7th.

She was one of the greatest queens to rule England and tudor England during these tudor times.

She was one of the best queens to rule Tudor England during the times of Anne Boleyn.

The life and times of Anne Boleeyn

The times of Anne Boleyn took a long time to heel during the times of Tudor England and during these tudor times.

Anne Boleyn and her final battle.

She was one of the best queens of England.

She was one of the greatest queens of Tudor England.
She graced England to become queen of England during Tudor times.
She faced her final battle and then her final hours before she was executed. On the 19th of May 1536.

Anne Boleyn' Final Days

Henry planned her death as the execution went ahead as the burning of Anne Boleyn did not happen and the execution took place instead as Henry was "kind" to he as he stopped the burning of her body taking place.

The final days of Anne Boleyn took place as the way the trail was true as the execution was controversial as the facts where quite true to this day as the execution took place on the 19th of May 1536.

The final days of Anne Boleyn were quite true as the facts where true as the memories of Anne Boleyn as she was killed on Tower hill outside the tower of London.

The way the odds where quite put against her as she was sadly put to death and executed instead of been burnt to death.

A specialist swordsman was brought in from France to carry out the beheading in a quicker way.

The way Henry ordered the execution of Anne Boleyn and not the burning of her body was quite kind, by Tudor standards, in the end.

Anne final days where quite different as she was a good queen of England

She was killed by a sword.

Anne Boleyn was   one of the best queens of Tudor England and in Tudor times.

She defended her rights to be queen of England and in Tudor times and in Tudor England.

She was one of the most famous and dedicated to the job of been queen of England and in Tudor times and in Tudor England.

Henry was not happy as been married to Anne Boleyn his decisions about the marriage to Anne Boleyn was quite difficult along the way to the execution of Anne Boleyn on the 19th of May 1536.

Henry should have been more loyal to Anne Boleyn he should have saved her from been executed in my opinion. But this sadly did not happen what shame this did happen

The final days of Anne Boleyn where quite hard to follow as the future of Anne Boleyn   defended herself before she was executed on the 19th of May 1536. It is nearly 884 years she died date of 19th of May 1536.

Anne legacy is quite hard to imagine as the song but John Lennon as her life was

 Short when she became queen of England during the times of the Tudors the reign of henry the 8th was very different after Anne was killed and executed the memories of her the execution should have nit have happened in, my opinion

The life and times of Anne Boleyn was quite hard to follow as the world of the Tudors whew quite difficult to enjoy life as been a Tudor as the legacy of Anne Boleyn what she died to defend the royal realms of the land.

Conclusion

I have been interested in Anne Boleyn for a long time I am really interested in History I studied history at Middlewich County high school from 1984-1989 she would be a good subject to study at across the education sector as mental health and history mix well together I think that Anne Boleyn was a very good queen of England and during the Tudor Dynasty as Henry failed to have an heir to the throne as he always wanted a son to be king after he died. Sometimes we don't really get what we want in life. As we sometimes do other things in our life time.